Korean Futures: Challenges to U.S. Diplomacy of North Korean Regime Collapse

Korean Futures: Challenges to U.S. Diplomacy of North Korean Regime Collapse

By Ferial Ara Saeed and James J. Przystup

Institute for National Strategic Studies
Strategic Perspectives, No. 7

Series Editors: Nicholas Rostow and Phillip C. Saunders

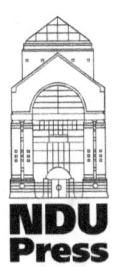

National Defense University Press
Washington, D.C.
September 2011

First printing, September 2011

For current publications of the Institute for National Strategic Studies, please go to the National Defense University Web site at: www.ndu.edu/inss.

Contents

Executive Summary

There is no shortage of plausible scenarios describing North Korean regime collapse or how the United States and North Korea's neighbors might respond to such a challenge. Yet comparatively little attention has been paid to the strategic considerations that may shape the responses of the United States, the Republic of Korea (ROK), Japan, China, and Russia to a North Korean crisis. These states are most likely to take action of some kind in the event the North Korean regime collapses. For the ROK (South Korea), North Korean regime collapse presents the opportunity for Korean reunification. For the other states, the outcome in North Korea will affect their influence on the peninsula and their relative weight in Asia. This study identifies the interests and objectives of these principal state actors with respect to the Korean Peninsula. Applying their interests and objectives to a generic scenario of North Korean regime collapse, the study considers possible policies that the principal state actors might use to cope with such a crisis.

The goal of this study is to motivate policymakers to consider how the United States would respond to regime collapse, not to identify the most plausible scenario. It is the pre-crisis planning process that is necessary in order to develop a comprehensive understanding of the issues, choices, and priorities that will challenge U.S. diplomacy in the event of North Korean regime collapse. In particular, Washington must plan for the likelihood that while the United States and South Korea will seek to be the primary actors in a crisis induced by North Korean regime collapse, the actions of China and North Korea will profoundly influence U.S. decisions and room to maneuver. The United States will also need to gain the cooperation of Japan and Russia, as well as the support of the United Nations, to achieve politically acceptable outcomes.

Regime collapse in North Korea is unlikely, especially in view of China's interest in preserving North Korea as a viable government and state. If it were to take place, however, North Korean regime collapse could fundamentally alter the strategic landscape in Asia, potentially in ways that would diminish U.S. influence in the region. Reduced American influence would constitute a serious, adverse turn of events for the United States. Asia is home to rising powers with which Washington must cooperate to set the global agenda in the 21st century. Continued American ability to shape the Asian strategic landscape will constitute a measure of U.S. power in the future and will be fundamental to achieving global stability, security, and prosperity.

The findings of this study highlight the complexities and dilemmas the United States would confront in a North Korean regime collapse crisis. First and foremost, the study emphasizes that regime collapse does not mean state collapse, at least not in the short run. China will seek to keep regime collapse from becoming state collapse—the end of the North Korean state. The international community also will not endorse ending the North Korean state without the support of a North Korean majority. In fact, North Korean cooperation will be more critical to the achievement of U.S. and ROK goals than has been previously appreciated.

Second, China will be in the most powerful position to act because it will likely be the first state in the region to become aware of a regime collapse crisis, having the best "eyes and ears" inside North Korea through its extensive commercial and diplomatic presence as well as pervasive party-to-party and military-to-military ties. China also will be the least conflicted among states in the region in its priorities, unlike the United States and South Korea. Without a guarantee that a unified Korea or a North Korea free of weapons of mass destruction (WMD) would be politically inclined toward China, Beijing will not support ROK and U.S. intervention aimed at reunification or WMD elimination. In seeking to constrain U.S. and ROK actions on the peninsula, China may find an ally in Russia. At the same time, Russia is likely to use the crisis to try to expand its influence in the region at China's expense.

Third, in this complicated environment of clashing interests and competing priorities, there is great potential for serious damage to U.S.-China relations, and misunderstandings and unmet expectations could create long-term problems for U.S. alliances with the ROK and Japan.

Washington will need to make momentous and difficult decisions: whether to intervene in North Korea and under what auspices and for what ends; and when to introduce the North Korea issue into the United Nations Security Council, to name a few. While making these difficult decisions, the United States will simultaneously be undertaking sensitive diplomatic and political tasks: taking steps to avoid creating an adversarial relationship with China while deterring Beijing from intervening militarily in North Korea, and possibly seeking congressional support for outcomes Washington judges to be less than ideal. Failure to gain strong bipartisan support for U.S. policy could undermine diplomacy with the ROK, China, Russia, Japan, and North Korea.

The realism and skill of U.S. diplomacy in the face of a North Korean regime collapse could determine the future of U.S. leadership in Asia and, in any event, will affect any resultant reshuffling of the strategic landscape in that region. It therefore is essential that Washington consider today how best to position the U.S. Government to respond intelligently to what could be the most serious challenge America has faced in Asia since the Vietnam War.

What I fear is not the enemy's strategy, but our mistakes.
—Thucydides[1]

Introduction

Regime collapse in North Korea will be a defining moment for U.S. leadership in Asia and a defining event for the region. Prospects for U.S.-China confrontation and for significant damage to U.S. alliances with the Republic of Korea (ROK) and Japan will be high. Interests, alignments, and relationships among the states in Northeast Asia may change. Reshuffling of the strategic landscape will be driven by the outcome on the peninsula and the role Washington played in achieving it, and also by the state of U.S. relations post-crisis with the ROK, Japan, and China. As a consequence, interaction between the United States and the ROK during the crisis, and the effectiveness with which the two states individually and together as allies shape and respond to Chinese actions, will be especially critical determinants of the strategic endstate in Asia.

Given these high stakes, it is imperative that Washington defines the principles that will guide U.S. diplomacy in a Korean contingency. To date, however, Washington has not developed a diplomatic framework for responding to North Korean regime collapse, presumably because fundamental interests of both the United States and important regional actors are at stake, and it is difficult to sort out the clashing interests and competing priorities of all the principal state actors. In addition, a diplomatic framework is scenario-dependent, and it is impossible to predict the unique combination of internal and external pressures that may cause the regime in Pyongyang to fall. Nonetheless, diplomatic planning is essential to the success of any humanitarian and military intervention contemplated by the U.S.–ROK alliance, and it is crucial to orchestrating endstates acceptable to the United States and the ROK.

This paper seeks to frame the issues, choices, and priorities that will challenge U.S. diplomacy in the event of North Korean regime collapse. A generic scenario of protracted instability in North Korea is used to illuminate the challenges the United States will face. The goal of this paper is not to predict the future by attempting to identify the most plausible regime collapse scenario. The goal is rather to provide a framework of analysis and motivate policymakers to start considering how the United States would respond to regime collapse and to organize bureaucratic resources accordingly.

It must be emphasized that regime collapse is a remote possibility. If it were to occur, however, it would be immensely challenging because North Korea is a nuclear weapons–capable state, and a rising Asia is critically important to U.S. national interests. Pre-crisis planning should consider how best to advance and protect a range of U.S. national interests during a regime collapse crisis, but this process will not produce a plan that can be dusted off and applied in an actual crisis, which is likely to unfold in ways not predicted by any scenario. It is the process itself that is useful. Organizing the U.S. Government to think through the issues will illuminate the range of actions to be considered no matter what type of crisis occurs.

This paper begins with our Key Findings. These are the major judgments we derived from considering both the interests and objectives of the principal state actors, and how these interests and objectives might influence their policy decisions in responding to the generic scenario of North Korean regime collapse presented later in the paper. Following the Key Findings is the first section of the paper, which presents the interests and priorities of the principal state actors in the crisis. This section is derived from extensive interviews with experts and former government officials, chiefly from South Korea and the United States,[2] as well as the authors' combined expertise on Asia, and a review of relevant academic studies on North Korean regime collapse, North Korea's relations with the principal state actors, reunification in other parts of the world, and studies on crisis response.

The next section of the paper sets forth a generic scenario of regime collapse in North Korea and the likely responses of the principal state actors to this scenario, based on their interests and objectives, as laid out in the first section of the paper. This section also describes the context for responding to North Korean regime collapse—both the likely venues for decision and dialogue, and the possible rationales for intervention. Following this section is a brief discussion of the relevance of our Key Findings to other possible scenarios of North Korean regime collapse. The final section of the paper presents policy recommendations, the steps the United States can take to plan for a highly complex diplomatic undertaking that may result in military intervention.

Key Findings

Sudden collapse of the Democratic People's Republic of Korea (DPRK) regime will not end North Korea as a state, at least not in the short run, because China is not likely to permit this result.

- The North Korean ruling elite will take all available measures to ensure state survival—state survival equals their survival.

- The ROK, Japan, China, and Russia will seek to contain the crisis inside North Korea in order to prevent an international crisis.

- China will seek to perpetuate the North Korean state as a buffer against a democratic-capitalist ROK allied with the United States.

- The international community will not endorse ending the North Korean state unless supported by a North Korean majority.

- The United States cannot stage-manage regime collapse.

- We have little knowledge about North Korea, limited access to its leadership, and even less access to its people.

- China will be the first to perceive a leadership crisis in North Korea and will intervene diplomatically to structure a successor regime—likely from among the current ruling elite.

- China or the United States will move the issue to the United Nations (UN) Security Council in order to constrain the other's actions and seek legitimacy for intervention. Debate will be hard to manage and could move in diversionary directions, but keeping the issue out of the UN as the ROK wants is unwise and unrealistic.

- Any intervention requires North Korean cooperation, which may be withheld.

- Key decisions will be: whether to intervene, who will intervene, under what auspices, and for what ends—humanitarian relief, weapons of mass destruction (WMD) elimination, WMD disaster (nuclear, chemical, biological), stabilization, or reunification.

Decisions on intervention and endstates—if they are mishandled—could risk U.S. influence and leadership in Asia.

- China will try to avoid provoking ROK–U.S. military intervention, and vice versa. However, preemptive intervention is possible by either side to prevent the other from intervening. The risk of miscalculation will be high. China may try to cooperate with the ROK to outmaneuver the United States.

- The endstates of U.S. bilateral relationships with the ROK, Japan, and China will be as important to American interests as the endstate on the peninsula.

- U.S. national security interests mandate WMD elimination, but U.S. intervention will be practically difficult and politically problematic, including for our allies.

- Absent the support of the ROK and China, the United States will find it difficult if not impossible to move forces north for a WMD mission. The ROK sequences WMD elimination after reunification and fears U.S. military intervention before reunification would only encourage Chinese military intervention.

- China and Russia are more concerned about preventing U.S. unilateralism than about WMD elimination. They likely will press for international monitoring, using the 2005 Joint Statement to demand *peaceful* denuclearization.

- Japan would like the United States to eliminate North Korean WMD but will hesitate to support Washington considering the risk of Chinese and Russian overreaction to U.S. troops near their borders, which could have devastating consequences for the region and for the U.S.-Japan alliance.

- Humanitarian intervention will resonate positively at the UN.

- Food aid will contain the crisis inside the DPRK and initially will be the ROK's primary tool to cope with the crisis.

- A refugee crisis would hit China hardest because of its long, permeable border with North Korea. Such a crisis could provide China with a basis for intervention.

- Humanitarian issues will be attractive and necessary areas for U.S.-China cooperation. Discussions to manage the risk of a tuberculosis pandemic could begin in the Strategic and Economic dialogue. North Korea has the highest tuberculosis infection rate outside sub-Saharan Africa, and the disease is multidrug resistant. If tuberculosis spread through Asia, the health and economic costs would be severe.

- Economic issues provide another possible arena for U.S.-China cooperation, especially joint efforts to encourage economic reforms that can "graduate" North Korea from requiring humanitarian assistance to just needing development aid.

U.S. diplomatic goals:

- deny a return to the pre-crisis political and WMD status quo

- ensure that the ROK and Japan are not vulnerable to Chinese pressure

- deter China from intervening militarily

- avoid creating an adversarial relationship with China

- steer the ROK into a lead role on humanitarian intervention

- exploit all opportunities to maneuver the ROK into an *overall leading role*

- manage ROK and Japanese expectations of the United States

- shape the UN process to maximize U.S.–ROK flexibility

- avoid actions that force North Korea into greater dependence on China

- frustrate any effort to characterize reunification as regime change

- prevent frictions based on different priorities among Northeast Asian states from permanently undermining U.S. relationships with those states.

Interests and Priorities of Principal State Actors

This section discusses the interests and priorities of the principal state actors that should apply in any North Korean crisis scenario. To provide a context for the following discussion, however, it is useful to describe in brief the generic scenario presented later in the paper. This generic scenario falls between an orderly rejection of Kim Jong-eun (Kim Jong-il's designated heir) by other members of the senior leadership and a more cataclysmic breakdown of central leadership provoking a civil war. The generic scenario in this paper is based on an orderly rejection of Kim Jong-eun. While the new leadership is culled from among the current ruling elite, the family of the founder of the North Korean state, Kim Il-sung, is out of power. The new leadership therefore is concerned about the loyalty of officials in the core institutions of the state, especially the military. North Korea's new leaders are seeking to control the armed forces. They confront an acceleration in the breakdown of the public distribution system. This breakdown poses a serious challenge for the new government because, while it has reestablished political authority and military control over a majority of North Korean provinces, in order to assert authority over the entire state it must repair and restore the public distribution system to full operations. Regime collapse, defined as the end of Kim Il-sung's dynasty, thus is distinct from state collapse, defined as the end of the North Korean state—the state has not collapsed.

Principal State Actors

Primary state actors in any North Korean regime collapse crisis will be the United States, South Korea, the DPRK, the People's Republic of China (PRC), Japan, and Russia (hereinafter referred to as the "Principal States").[3] These states are participants in the Six Party Talks process. They have the largest stake in the outcome of a regime collapse crisis. For the ROK, North Korean regime collapse presents an opportunity for Korean reunification, and for the other Principal States, the outcome in North Korea will affect their influence on the peninsula and their relative weight in Asia. Equally important in motivating their concern over events in North Korea is concern that they also could be drawn into a wider conflict if there are massive refugee outflows from North Korea. This anxiety is particularly true for China, which has the longest and most porous border with North Korea.

There is a hierarchy of relevance among the Principal States. The United States and South Korea will play critical roles throughout the crisis as allies. Washington and Seoul will be most affected by the actions of North Korea and China, allies (in the narrowest sense of the term) with a strongly shared stake in the perpetuation of the North Korean state. Decisions made in the United States, South Korea, North Korea, and China, therefore, will determine the course of the crisis, and how prolonged and violent it is.

Japan and Russia will play roles of varying significance as events unfold. For instance, assuming action moves to the United Nations, Russia will play a more prominent role as a permanent member of the Security Council. If the U.S.-Japan alliance declares SIASJ (Situations in Areas Surrounding Japan under the 1997 Defense Guidelines),[4] Japan's role will rise in prominence.

Ordering of Principal State Priorities

The Principal States (minus North Korea) will share an initial focus on the humanitarian dimensions of the crisis. This humanitarian focus will resonate at the UN. For South Korea, the United States, and China, humanitarian concerns may become a pretext for intervention. However, it will be difficult to move from intervention to achieve humanitarian goals to an intervention that seeks to achieve political ends. As a consequence, while the Principal States will share an initial humanitarian focus and a general desire to contain and stabilize the crisis inside North Korea, concern over the endstate on the peninsula and the potential need for intervention to achieve political ends will cause each state to order its top priorities in the crisis differently.

The United States: (1) Pursue WMD elimination and prevent proliferation, (2) contain and stabilize the crisis inside North Korea, (3) incline the North Korean leadership toward the United States and the ROK to support ROK-led reunification, and (4) preserve Asian alliances and cooperation with China.

ROK: (1) Contain and stabilize the crisis inside North Korea while preventing outside (PRC and U.S.) intervention, (2) incline the DPRK leadership toward the ROK, preparing the way for reunification, (3) eliminate WMD during reunification, and (4) preserve alliance with United States while ensuring cooperative relations with China.

China: (1) Contain and stabilize the crisis inside North Korea, (2) preserve North Korea as an independent state and deter U.S.–ROK intervention, (3) incline the DPRK leadership toward China and ensure the new regime adopts Chinese-style economic reform, (4) bring North Korean WMD programs under international monitoring, and (5) preserve cooperation with the United States.

Japan: (1) Contain and stabilize the crisis inside North Korea, (2) prevent PRC intervention, (3) eliminate WMD and prevent proliferation, (4) defer a SIASJ declaration, (5) ensure that Japan has a say on the endstate on the peninsula, and (6) preserve alliance with the United States while ensuring cooperative relations with China.

Russia: (1) Contain and stabilize the crisis inside North Korea while deterring U.S.–ROK and PRC intervention, (2) maximize opportunities for Russia to expand its influence in Asia and global role, and its influence on the endstate on the peninsula; and (3) bring North Korean WMD programs under international monitoring.

A discussion of the priorities of the Principal States follows.

U.S. Priorities

For six decades, reducing tension on the Korean Peninsula and promoting peaceful re-unification have been intimately tied to the paramount U.S. national security interest of maintaining peace and stability in Asia. U.S. alliances with Japan and South Korea have been the cornerstone of this policy.

Over the past two decades, the acceleration of the North Korean nuclear program has starkly focused U.S. policymakers on a narrow but substantial set of dangers posed by a nuclear weapons–capable North Korea that is actively proliferating WMD and missile technology. North Korea's WMD and missile cooperation with states in the Middle East and Southwest Asia is destabilizing to U.S. interests in these regions and poses a threat to U.S. national security. Since the threat North Korea poses has expanded beyond Asia, Washington no longer appears to define North Korea as a peninsula problem but rather as a global WMD and proliferation problem. By contrast, the principal states continue to see North Korea as a peninsula problem with a nuclear dimension. Managing these divergent definitions of the North Korea problem has posed a challenge to U.S. diplomacy, a challenge that will grow more difficult in a regime collapse crisis.

The apparent change in the way Washington defines the problem means the most important U.S. objective during a North Korean regime collapse crisis will be to eliminate or otherwise greatly reduce the threat posed by North Korea's WMD and missile programs and proliferation activities—likely packaged as the necessary prelude to reunification. Proliferation concerns will drive Washington toward military intervention to secure the North Korean arsenal. A major obstacle to this effort, however, will be ROK concerns that U.S. intervention to secure WMD would provide Beijing a pretext for military intervention. Absent the support of China and the ROK, the United States will find it difficult, if not impossible, to move forces into North Korea for a WMD mission. Even if circumstances permitted U.S. military intervention, the operational difficulties of attempting to secure North Korean WMD could be overwhelming in the likely event of North Korean opposition and outright resistance. Washington will be forced to consider other, more realistic policy options.

ROK Priorities

North Korean regime collapse would present a historic opportunity for reunification and for ridding South Korea of its most significant security threat. Whether the Blue House would seize the opportunity for reunification will depend on the government in power. A progressive

ROK government would probably not be inclined to pursue reunification, while a conservative Blue House might be inclined to make the attempt. An additional component of the internal ROK debate will be the recognition that Seoul's resources are limited and that any final resolution to the problem would require considerable international assistance as well as international acceptance and recognition of new borders.

Even if the Blue House favored a particular policy course, moreover, deep and predictable divisions in the ROK political landscape—along ideological, generational, and regional lines—will surface during the contingency. Pressures from inside the ROK government, particularly from within the ROK military, also will push the Blue House toward (or away from) reunification, regardless of who occupies the presidency—a progressive or conservative. The Blue House thus will be forced into making historically significant policy decisions without strong public consensus. In this weak domestic political context, Seoul will look to Washington for support.

The initial ROK objective will be to contain and stabilize the situation, possibly through food aid alone, without intervening inside North Korea. If the situation stabilizes and the Chinese stay out of North Korea, the Blue House would need to develop a package of steps for eventual reunification to demonstrate that it did not allow an opportunity to slip by to unify the peninsula. If the situation remains unstable or if the Chinese seem poised to intervene, debate in Seoul would become even more contentious, divided over the merits of intervention versus relying on nonmilitary stabilization measures.

In the context of Seoul struggling with these momentous and difficult policy decisions regarding the future of the Korean Peninsula, introducing the question of U.S. intervention to eliminate WMD will highlight our fundamental differences regarding the disposition of North Korean WMD. Seoul believes WMD elimination should be deferred to the final stage of reunification. While Seoul has sound operational arguments in defense of this sequencing of events, it may wish to keep open the option of retaining WMD capability after reunification. Moreover, for South Korea, removing the conventional military threat North Korea poses is far more important because that would materially improve ROK security.

ROK views on the pace of reunification have evolved since the end of the Korean War. The central question of whether to "take over" North Korea quickly or opt for a gradual "merger" has essentially been decided in favor of a "takeover" for the following reasons: (1) to preempt Chinese influence from severely setting back ROK influence in a united Korea; (2) to apply the lessons of the German experience, which remains a model for the ROK despite significant differences in the two cases;[5] and (3) to ensure the wholesale and most expeditious transplantation of ROK institutions into the DPRK. Gradualism risks the infiltration of socialist institutions and ideology from North Korea into South Korea. Whether a takeover is realistic, however, is another question that would become a major topic of debate during a North Korean crisis.

Seoul will expect unwavering U.S. support as it seeks to carve out a role of leadership in the crisis, especially in dealing with issues related to intervention and the endstate on the peninsula. However, existing legal instruments supporting ROK objectives—the ROK constitution, the Armistice Agreement, and UN resolutions dating back to 1948—will be subject to challenge or different interpretation by China and North Korea, and potentially by other UN member states. Separate ROK and DPRK UN membership facilitates arguments that the UN should acknowledge and affirm the interests of the North Korean state.

China's Priorities

Stability on China's periphery is important to continued Chinese economic growth and development, which, in turn, is essential to the continued legitimacy of the Communist Party leadership and PRC regime stability. Instability in North Korea would be bad for business in China and therefore threaten core Chinese national interests. Thus, initially, Beijing's primary goals will be to stabilize the situation inside North Korea and prevent a refugee crisis. However, regime collapse in North Korea will offer China the unique opportunity to remake North Korea in China's image, something Beijing has failed to do so far.

North Korea as it is today is a limited but still significant asset to China.[6] The DPRK provides the PRC a buffer against a democratic Korea allied to the United States[7] and a source of raw materials, warm water ports, and, potentially, markets for Chinese goods. North Korea's limited nuclear capability poses few risks to Chinese interests and gives Pyongyang bargaining leverage that indirectly accrues to Beijing as North Korea's protector.[8] Given these existing advantages, a North Korea transformed into China's image and integrated into the Chinese economy would be an immense asset to the PRC. In recent years, Beijing has invested considerable resources to secure a strong foothold in North Korea through a relatively robust commercial presence and extensive official engagement at multiple levels. Beijing links access to North Korean ports and resources to the development of China's northeastern provinces. More importantly for the Chinese leadership, North Korean economic development would mean stability at China's periphery.

While China's core national interests will be at risk if North Korea becomes unsustainable as a state, the leadership will avoid any long-term entanglement in the DPRK that exhausts Chinese resources and risks a political backlash at home. Rather, China will aim for a minimum presence of a duration sufficient to stabilize the situation consonant with core PRC national interests.[9]

China will remain reluctant to engage in discussions with the United States on North Korea. First and foremost, Beijing distrusts Washington's strategic intentions and does not care to tip its hand, suspicious that the United States seeks to constrain China's emergence as a great power. In addition, China cannot afford to alienate North Korea, part of its periphery. At the same time, stable post-crisis U.S.-China relations are in China's long-term interest, and Beijing will look for ways to cooperate with the United States.

China also will seek to protect its relationship with the ROK, which is deep and extensive on the economic side. This relationship sustained serious damage when China failed to condemn the DPRK in 2010 both for sinking the ROK naval frigate, the *Cheonan*, and for firing on Yeonpyeong Island.

Last but not least, PRC leaders will be concerned about the "reputational costs" of saving the North Korean state, which under present conditions offers the region nothing but security challenges and the potential for instability. China therefore will emphasize the principle of protecting the rights of a sovereign state. Tensions between the United States and China over the structure of regional security are likely to arise in the context of outcomes on the peninsula. There may be outcomes short of reunification that would allow the United States to adjust its commitments and deployments in the region, such as a WMD- and missile-free North Korea with a sharply reduced conventional military posture that, therefore, poses a significantly reduced threat to Seoul and Tokyo. However, it is hard to imagine any outcome that would convince the United States to shed its commitments and deployments altogether, at least not anytime soon.

Japan's Priorities

Under ordinary circumstances, regime collapse in North Korea would pose an extremely difficult challenge to Japan. Were it to occur over the next several years, however, the challenge would be exponentially more difficult as Japan also copes with rebuilding from the devastation of the March 2011 tsunami.

Like the other Principal States, Japan initially will support efforts to contain and stabilize the crisis inside North Korea. Tokyo's longer term interests lie in emerging from the crisis with the U.S. presence on the peninsula intact, so that Japan is not alone in hosting U.S. troops in the region. In addition, Japan will likely seek greater influence on the peninsula and in the region, especially at China's expense, as well as improved relations with South Korea. Tokyo will work toward shaping events and outcomes in the direction of a WMD-free peninsula. There will be a high likelihood throughout the contingency of unfulfilled demands and expectations by the United States and Japan that, unchecked, will undermine confidence in the alliance.

Japan will regard an endstate on the peninsula in which China has the upper hand as inimical to Japanese interests. Tokyo therefore will support efforts by the United States and the ROK to prevent PRC intervention during the crisis. On the other hand, Korean reunification evokes Japanese ambivalence, although it is not an outcome Japan can or would try to prevent. Reunification raises serious questions about whether the ROK will continue to be host to a substantial U.S. force presence.[10] In the longer term, a weak but unified Korea, focused on internal reconstruction, will make Japan the strongest state in the region confronting a rising China—not a position in which Tokyo will be comfortable. Finally, unless historic Japan-Korea animosities are reduced, Japan will be concerned about how a unified Korea and Japan will interact. At the same time, ROK support for Japan since the March 2011 tsunami provides an important building block for improved bilateral ROK-Japan relations.

Russia's Priorities

Russia's core interest is to regain relevance and prestige in Asia, a region Moscow recognizes as growing in global importance. All possible avenues to showcase Russia's global and regional importance will be exploited. For instance, Moscow will use the contingency to highlight U.S.-Russian cooperation on humanitarian endeavors to contain and stabilize the crisis. Russia also may use the opportunity of the crisis to strengthen relations with China. On the issue of U.S. intervention for a WMD mission, moreover, Russia likely will side with China and insist on peaceful resolution.[11] Like China, Russia seeks to constrain U.S. unilateralism and does not perceive North Korean WMD to be sufficiently threatening to Russian interests to move beyond calling for peaceful denuclearization. It is important to emphasize that while Russia strongly supports a denuclearized Korean Peninsula, Moscow consistently underscores that this outcome must be achieved peacefully, through nonmilitary means.[12]

Russia and China share key interests in North Korea and may seek to cooperate to constrain the United States and the ROK. However, Russia also seeks to undercut China's influence on the peninsula and in the region, and may attempt to exploit divisions between China and the ROK, and China and the DPRK. Russia, therefore, will strongly support referring the matter to the UN, where Moscow can maximize its influence as a veto-wielding permanent member of the Security Council and otherwise seek to constrain the actions of China, the United States, and South Korea. At the same time, good relations with both Koreas are important to Moscow as it looks ahead to securing Russian influence on the peninsula. Russia also has important commercial ties to South Korea. Just as China seeks to harness the North Korean economy to its northeastern provinces, so Russia seeks to harness the economy of the Russian Far East to North Korea.

Venues for Decision and Dialogue

United Nations

The UN Security Council will be the primary venue for discussions and decisions during the crisis. Using the UN for these purposes will be a serious bone of contention between the United States and the ROK. Seoul expects Washington to manage Beijing and legitimize ROK–U.S. military intervention without recourse to the UN. However, military intervention without UN endorsement would be unwise and politically difficult to manage. The United States and South Korea would be vulnerable to charges of seeking regime change if they intervened militarily without UN cover. While China has recourse to the 1961 DPRK-China security treaty (discussed below) and can claim to be "invited in," the same cannot be said of the United States and South Korea. Moreover, the United States and China can best constrain one another in the Security Council, which makes it an important venue for managing the crisis and achieving U.S. and ROK objectives. That said, both the UN General Assembly (UNGA) and the Security Council will become liabilities to the United States if international support for ROK–U.S. intervention is lacking. Debate at the UN will also be hard to manage. Issues may be raised that divert attention from U.S. goals. Seoul fears China will exercise its veto and severely constrain ROK actions, demonstrating in the process that Beijing has the upper hand over Seoul—a fact North Korean elites would duly note. The UN as a venue for decisionmaking will become a source of strain in the alliance.

If Washington takes the North Korea issue to the UN before Beijing does so, the United States can constrain Chinese actions in the DPRK. For example, by refusing to recognize any PRC-installed DPRK regime and declaring it "provisional," Washington could buy time and possibly the opportunity to capitalize on events inside North Korea that may unfold in ways beneficial to the United States. The main disadvantage of acting first early in the crisis is that Washington may force Beijing into a hard defense of the DPRK, which could reduce room to negotiate issues related to endstates.

Regional Venues for Dialogue

To underscore the regional nature of the U.S. approach to the crisis and to conduct useful consultations with those states with a clear stake in the outcome on the peninsula, the United States will seek to convene the Principal States (probably minus North Korea) under the framework of the Six Party Talks. The purpose would be to discuss the crisis rather than WMD issues, although that subject would be a component of talks. China will be reluctant to go along, not wanting to alienate or further isolate the regime in Pyongyang, and Beijing is not likely to share its own goals or plans for responding to the crisis. However, convening a Six Party meeting will put some pressure on China, while reminding the international community of understandings previously reached in the Six Party process on WMD issues. China and Russia will seek to underscore the principle of peaceful denuclearization in the 2005 Joint Statement. The United States, South Korea, and Japan will meet trilaterally to project alignment among the allies, further underscoring the regional nature of the crisis response. These meetings will not satisfy Japan's demands for consultation and reassurance, but will demonstrate that Japan is playing a role in the crisis.

Bilateral Venues for Dialogue

In any North Korean crisis, the ROK can best be positioned to assume a leading role if Seoul is assertive and proactive on humanitarian issues early on, possibly even approaching the UN Secretary General for aid to North Korea. At a minimum, the ROK could be in visible talks with the European Union, the Association of Southeast Asian Nations, and even Japan regarding contributions to humanitarian relief and for longer term commitments to North Korea. Actions of this kind will not guarantee South Korea a lead role in the crisis, but they could significantly shift the odds in Seoul's favor by giving it a prominent and important platform from which to claim a larger leadership role.

The United States has two channels for direct contact with North Korea: through the DPRK mission to the UN in New York and the Military Armistice Commission at Panmunjom. Both channels would be kept open during the crisis, recognizing, however, that they may be corrupted by groups representing independent factions or otherwise unable to speak authoritatively for the new regime. It may be useful to establish alternative channels through the DPRK missions in Vienna, Bern, and Geneva. (Risk of monitoring by third countries would need to be taken into account.)

Rationales for Intervention

ROK Constitution

To justify intervention, South Korea will point to Article III of its constitution, which claims the entire peninsula to be under ROK administration. Seoul believes that this provision offers sufficient political cover for any type of intervention, military or humanitarian. However, the rationale of Article III is not likely to persuade an international community that recognizes North Korea as a separate state. Russia and China, moreover, have treaties with the DPRK that would make it difficult to support or allow coercive dissolution of the North Korean state. Another option is for the ROK to approach the UN Secretary General for humanitarian aid under Article III, thereby establishing a precedent for acceptance of Article III. However, this is just as likely to backfire and result in a challenge from the DPRK (whose constitution claims to represent all Koreans) and possibly from China.[13]

The Armistice

Reasserting the political authority and operational lead of the ROK–U.S. alliance enshrined in the United Nations Command and the Military Armistice Commission structures may maximize U.S.–ROK flexibility at the UN. The United States could approach the Security Council in its capacity as head of the UN Command and, referencing UN Security Council Resolution 85,[14] seek political cover for ROK forces crossing into the DPRK to provide a safe and secure environment for the delivery of humanitarian aid (and the return of internally displaced persons and refugees). However, the UN Command has been operating independently of the UN; therefore, reasserting its linkage to the UN will be challenging and may have negative consequences in terms of UN mission management.

More importantly, the Armistice is clear that the military of one side may cross into the other's territory *only* with the permission of the receiving command. The United States would need to declare the other command incapable of speaking for the DPRK. Having alternative bilateral channels to North Korea through its missions in European capitals could prove useful in that regard. Armistice Article IV, point 60 calls for "peaceful settlement of the Korean question." If the new DPRK regime cannot control its borders and internal violence causes people to flee, this situation would constitute a threat to ROK security, providing a rationale for intervention. The important point here is that developing a rationale for intervention will require a thorough understanding of existing agreements and mechanisms as well as the risks of invoking and applying them.

UN Security Council Resolutions

The UN Charter is exceedingly careful in its treatment of respect for "matters which are essentially within the domestic jurisdiction of any state," while reserving the responsibility of the Security Council to maintain or restore international peace and security.[15] In 2005, the UN General Assembly guardedly endorsed the "responsibility-to-protect."[16] This concept emphasizes the responsibility of states to protect their populations from genocide, war crimes, ethnic cleansing, and crimes against humanity.[17] The first application of responsibility-to-protect to justify military intervention was in UN Security Council Resolution 1973 on Libya (March 17, 2011). However, the invocation of responsibility-to-protect would potentially set back U.S. and ROK goals in the event of a North Korean regime collapse, and it is highly unlikely that China or Russia, both permanent members of the Security Council, would endorse its application to North Korea.

First, responsibility-to-protect requires that all other measures—a ceasefire, negotiation, and the use of economic and political incentives, for instance—be exhausted before resorting to military force, the last resort. China could make a good case for insisting on economic and political incentives, such as repairing the DPRK distribution system to contain an incipient humanitarian crisis, to help restore order, and to create the conditions for a negotiated end to any attacks on civilians by North Korean authorities. During the course of Security Council discussion on whether to invoke responsibility-to-protect, it would not be outside the realm of possibility for North Korea to threaten to use WMD against South Korea or Japan or to fire off missiles to "warn" the international community against military intervention. Even in the unlikely event that a resolution embracing responsibility-to-protect were passed because China and Russia abstained on the condition that a negotiated settlement would be attempted, it is hard to imagine Beijing and Moscow moving from this position to allowing the use of military force against North Korea.

Second, if responsibility-to-protect were invoked, how would the ROK and United States move from a humanitarian mandate for intervention to reunification or WMD elimination? There is already concern in the international community that powerful states will abuse responsibility-to-protect to justify interventions that serve their political interests rather than humanitarian goals.[18] This accusation could easily be leveled against South Korea if Seoul decided to seize the opportunity to pursue reunification during humanitarian intervention.

It is an accusation that could also be leveled against the United States. In fact, invoking responsibility-to-protect would complicate Washington's ability to work from humanitarian intervention to WMD elimination. Undertaking a separate WMD mission will rely on an entirely different set of UN resolutions, those condemning North Korea's WMD and proliferation activities, as the basis for U.S. intervention to secure and eliminate WMD programs. The WMD mission will also not be limited to intervening militarily in North Korea. It will include reinvigorating the Proliferation Security Initiative and adopting new UN Security

Council resolutions to close exit points from North Korea—requiring discussions at the UN that would open up the United States to charges of using responsibility-to-protect as cover for a political mission.

Third, it is unlikely that China or Russia would accept the application of responsibility-to-protect to North Korea for a variety of other reasons. China, in particular, consistently has supported negotiation over military intervention at the Security Council. In the case of Libya, both China and Russia abstained, apparently because of the support for intervention from the Arab League; however, both Moscow and Beijing issued statements "regretting" military action against Libya.[19] Russia and China likely will oppose intervention justified by responsibility-to-protect given that they consider their own human rights practices and other matters to be internal affairs.

1961 Sino-Korean Treaty

China has a solid legal rationale for intervention in North Korea under Article II of the Sino-Korean Treaty of Friendship, Cooperation, and Mutual Assistance. Article II states that in the event of an armed attack by any state or several states jointly against one of the Contracting Parties, the other would "immediately render military and other assistance by all means at its disposal." Moreover, Article VI states that Korean unification must be "peaceful and democratic," and in accordance with the "national interests of the Korean people." Thus, any ROK efforts toward reunification taking place under circumstances of disarray and chaos in the DPRK would be inconsistent with Article VI of this bilateral treaty, which could be cited by either China or the DPRK to challenge the ROK. In addition, Article V of this treaty underscores the principle of "mutual respect for sovereignty," making it difficult for China to support any effort coercively to dissolve the North Korean state or forcibly seize WMD facilities and stocks.

2000 Russia-DPRK Treaty

Similarly, under the Russia-DPRK Treaty of Friendship, Good Neighborliness, and Cooperation, both sides committed to develop relations on the principle of mutual respect for state sovereignty and territorial integrity. This fact will make it difficult for Russia to agree to any effort to dissolve coercively the North Korean state. Moreover, the treaty provides that in the event of a security emergency, both sides shall "enter into contact with each other immediately." This commitment preserves Russian flexibility on whether to provide military or other assistance to North Korea, and on whether to intervene in North Korea.

While Russia has had difficulty in reenergizing relations with North Korea, the 2000 Treaty gives Moscow a potentially important voice on decisions on intervention and the endstate in North Korea. It also is a lever that North Korea could use to temper Chinese influence or to force China to compete with Russia for influence—especially if North Korea invoked the Treaty's consultative mechanism and Russia agreed to talks. In that case, North Korea might seek to drive a deeper wedge between Washington and Moscow.

Korean Collapse Scenario

This section applies the foregoing discussion of interests and objectives of the Principal States to a generic scenario of regime collapse in North Korea. Under this generic scenario, the Kim regime falls as a result of challenge from within the current ruling elite, ending the dynasty of Kim Il-sung but not the North Korean state. A weak successor government politically supported by China and culled from the current ruling elite reestablishes a semblance of order. Scenarios based on rejection by North Koreans of the institutions of state were avoided because they make the decision to intervene too easy—more defensible politically because intervention would support internal actors seeking to change the regime. The generic scenario in this paper is not more plausible than others, but it is realistic and far more complex, encompassing the broadest possible range of issues, concerns, and political decisions. Above all, the critical decision on whether to intervene militarily would not be an easy or obvious choice.

Events within North Korea

In the scenario, a new government has reestablished political authority and military control over a majority of North Korean provinces but not the entire state. To consolidate its power and control over the state, the new regime is moving (1) to restore all significant economic activity to state control, (2) to gain control over the security and armed forces, and (3) to dominate public information media so that little information leaks in or out. The new government also faces an acceleration of existing challenges: the breakdown of the public distribution system intensifies, further weakening the state's economic and social control and generating small but growing populations of internally displaced persons and the potential for massive refugee outflows.

Woefully inadequate information undermines the ability of the United States to make plausible assessments about the possible trajectory of events. However, escalating refugee flows, largely into China, suggest a high risk for a wider conflict engulfing neighboring states. This risk is prompting consideration of humanitarian intervention to stabilize and contain the crisis inside North Korea.

North Korea's External Posture

The new government is focused on preserving the North Korean state at all costs. Pyong-yang will make its case to the UN, ask the Chinese to seek Security Council intervention, and/or invite China to intervene in order to stabilize the situation. North Koreans will not welcome ROK and/or U.S. military intervention, even for the purpose of distributing humanitarian aid, and neither state will be "invited in." The regime may invite China to intervene, but North Koreans over time will see the Chinese as an occupying force. A protracted Chinese military presence could rekindle historic Korean-Chinese hatred on both sides of the 38th parallel, presenting serious complications for the regime and for the Chinese.[20] In that case, the North Korean regime would need to weigh the political disadvantages of continued cooperation with China against the need to restore essential services, especially food distribution, to stabilize the country, especially if Chinese assistance in this area is not forthcoming or is ineffective or insufficient.

The new DPRK leadership will continue to project a profoundly anti-American posture and will find it useful politically to challenge the United States as the obstacle to Korean reunification, reprising a familiar theme in North Korean politics. Historic Korean distrust of China will temper the new leadership's willingness to confront Washington, unless the United States shows itself, through policy and public statements, to be antagonistic to the new regime. In addition, the DPRK desire to play the United States and China against each other will require pragmatism in North Korea's dealings with the two powers.

Republic of Korea's Response

ROK Policy Conflicted. The ROK government and body politic will be internally at odds in formulating a response to regime collapse in North Korea—divided over whether to stabilize and contain the crisis inside the state or to seize the opportunity to intervene militarily to lay the groundwork for reunification. Decisionmaking paralysis in Seoul will prompt the ROK to seek consultations with Washington, while facing tremendous pressure domestically to respond quickly enough to preempt Chinese military intervention.

ROK Concern over Chinese Influence. At the same time, China will be active in North Korea, driving Seoul to seek to minimize China's opportunities to enhance its position and ability to shape the future of the DPRK. Seoul's perception that China's role and influence in North Korea are increasing would provoke considerable concern within the government, particularly within the ROK military establishment. Washington will need to engage Seoul to check any tendencies to intervene preemptively with military force by reassuring South Korea that the United States will work to prevent China from dictating the outcome in North Korea.

ROK Leadership during the Crisis. Without question, ROK influence over events and the endstate in North Korea will be affected by China's role and by the extent to which South Korea must rely on international support. The more South Korea relies on international support to cope with the contingency, the weaker Seoul's influence will be on the endstate and inside North Korea. Washington will need to be mindful of these realities throughout the crisis to ensure that steps are taken whenever and wherever possible to position the ROK into a leading role.

China's Response

China Will Become Aware of Regime Collapse First. China will be in the most powerful position initially to influence events in North Korea and the least conflicted regarding the future of the North Korean state. It likely will be the first state in the region to realize that there is a leadership crisis in Pyongyang. China has a large diplomatic mission in North Korea with access to the top leadership. Party-to-party ties appear to be strong, as well as ties between the Korean People's Army and People's Liberation Army, and China's commercial interests are spread throughout the country. Perhaps no other state has better "eyes and ears" on the ground in North Korea than China. China has contingency plans to address instability in North Korea. Initial Chinese intervention, however, is likely to be political and diplomatic in nature.

China will move with great subtlety, at a pace dictated by opportunity and circumstance, but certainly rapidly enough to forestall a widening crisis—especially one that involves North Korean refugees spilling across the border into China. A refugee crisis would represent a failure of Chinese policy. Responding wisely to China's initial maneuvers inside North Korea will pose a key diplomatic challenge to the United States and South Korea. Washington will be at a disadvantage because Beijing will remain reluctant to engage in any but the most cursory discussions with the United States and the other Principal States regarding developments on the ground in North Korea and on North Korea's future. This Chinese attitude reflects underlying mistrust between the United States and China as well as China's desire not to alienate or further isolate the DPRK.

China Will Try to Delay UN Action until after a New DPRK Regime Is Installed. China is not likely to take the North Korea crisis to the Security Council until after a new regime is installed. It also will use all levers to prevent others from using UN fora to press for state collapse. If Washington tries to take the Korean crisis to the UN first, before Beijing is ready, that might position the United States to circumscribe China's diplomatic maneuvering in North Korea. However, U.S. flexibility would be reduced, and Washington would be at odds early on with Seoul, which opposes taking the North Korea issue to the UN. North Korea could appeal to the UN General Assembly on its own but is more likely to work through China for UN Security Council action, especially to preempt or stop ROK–U.S. military intervention or efforts to obtain Security Council action.

Ambiguous Chinese Posture on Reunification. China's goal is to preserve the North Korean state. To avoid uncomfortable parallels with Taiwan, however, the Chinese public posture on Korean reunification will be ambiguous—supportive of the concept, but under conditions that will be political nonstarters for the United States and possibly South Korea (such as withdrawal or severe downsizing of the U.S. military presence in the ROK).

Conditions Under Which the PRC Would Intervene Military. China will take the provocative step of military intervention under any of four conditions: (1) if the crisis cannot be contained inside North Korea through other measures, (2) if North Korean leaders appear to be losing control over the WMD and missile arsenal, (3) if the United States and/or South Korea intervene, or (4) if the United States and/or South Korea seem about to intervene (in which case China would intervene preemptively).

Advancing Long-term Interests. China could advance its long-term interests in a contingency with the following outcomes:

- China's ideal outcome is likely to be the preservation of a separate and stable North Korean state that adopts Chinese-style economic reforms, is integrated into the economies of China's northeastern provinces (Jilin, Heilongjiang, and Liaoning), and in which Chinese influence is preponderant. China may prefer a WMD-free North Korea but also believes North Korea's limited nuclear capability poses manageable risks to Chinese interests and may even confer certain strategic advantages: limited nuclear capability gives North Korea bargaining leverage in the region that indirectly accrues to China as Pyongyang's protector. Moreover, perpetuating the North Korean state offers China a continued physical and psychological buffer against the influences of a democratic Korea.

- Though of extremely low probability, another option entails the withdrawal of U.S. forces from the ROK and the expansion of Chinese influence across the peninsula. North Korean regime collapse would present China with the opportunity to insist that North Korea relinquish its nuclear capabilities as a condition of Chinese support for the continuation of the North Korean state, which would give China leverage against a continued U.S. presence in the ROK and possibly Japan. A denuclearized North Korea would mean a fundamentally transformed state, one potentially moving toward normal relations with Seoul, Washington, and Tokyo. China could exploit this new status quo to put pressure on a continued U.S. military presence on the peninsula and in Japan.

- Equally improbable is that Beijing could, with proper guarantees from South Korea regarding treatment of the North Korean leadership, structure an outcome that would result in both denuclearization and a path to unification—provided Seoul accepts an end to the U.S. presence on the peninsula. Strategically, this outcome would enhance China's standing in the region, incline a united Korea toward China, and put pressure on Japan as the last bastion of a U.S. military presence in Northeast Asia.

U.S. Response

U.S. Policy Conflicted. Politics in Washington will be polarized between those desiring to seize the opportunity to eliminate the North Korean WMD programs and effect regime change on the one hand, and those favoring stability and crisis containment on the other hand. One should anticipate congressional demands for sanctions against the new regime as a way to press for change. If adopted, sanctions would work at cross-purposes with efforts in the region to contain the crisis.

WMD Elimination. Absent North Korean cooperation, the United States stands to face serious opposition from the ROK and other states to attempt to eliminate North Korea's WMD. The other Principal States may resent the effort to achieve through military intervention what the United States failed to achieve through diplomacy. China and Russia would seek to defer decisions on the North Korean WMD programs until the political situation is more settled and the crisis contained. Moscow and Beijing are likely to insist on a peaceful, diplomatic resolution, such as international monitoring of the North Korean WMD programs—and would need to ensure North Korean cooperation. This outcome would not be welcome among Washington policymakers who have waited two decades for regime collapse and the opportunity to dismantle these programs.

Korean Reunification. With the support of China and Russia (and likely France and the United Kingdom), the United States can make denuclearization and reunification principal goals in a UN Security Council resolution. Whether Washington can intervene militarily to accomplish these objectives is another question. That will hinge on North Korean cooperation and the international community's perception of whether that cooperation is willing or coerced. If it appears to be coerced, the call for reunification may be seen as regime change by another name. Governments otherwise comfortable with ROK intervention to permit delivery of humanitarian aid, who generally oppose the DPRK's WMD capabilities and are thus willing to comply with UN resolutions and sanctions on North Korea, will not agree to overthrow the North Korean state. On the other hand, if North Korea complies with ROK–U.S. objectives, Washington will need to consider reassurances to China regarding the structure and positioning of U.S. forces in a unified peninsula as well as Korean commitments to drop irredentist claims previously made by both North and South Korea.

Relations with China. China's role in propping up the new North Korean regime will provoke significant political opposition in the United States that could, unchecked, undermine post-crisis U.S.-China relations. Both sides will seek to cooperate during the crisis in order to temper these negative impulses. Humanitarian issues will afford opportunities for U.S.-China cooperation: pandemic planning, negotiating secure access with North Korea for humanitarian relief organizations, and possibly, late in the crisis, initiatives that will promote economic reform.

Relations with the ROK. While the United States will not wish China to dictate the political future of North Korea, South Korea likely will not be able to determine North Korea's future. For the duration of the crisis, this likely reality will greatly complicate alliance relations. Both sides will need to work hard to prevent misunderstandings and disappointed expectations from causing longer term damage or drift in the alliance. It will be extremely important for the United States to avail itself of every opportunity to position South Korea, and support South Korea's positioning of itself, in a leading role in the crisis. At the same time, Washington will need to avoid being dragged into actions or postures by Seoul that will be inimical to U.S. and ROK interests over the long term.

Relations with Japan. Relations with Japan will suffer as a result of unmet expectations by both sides, as discussed below. Throughout the crisis, both Tokyo and Washington will need to undertake actions to prevent misunderstandings and disappointed expectations from causing longer term damage or drift in the alliance. For Washington, the challenge will be to demonstrate that the United States is doing its utmost to ensure that Tokyo's opinions count in the reckoning of the endstate on the peninsula and address other Japanese concerns without being dragged into endless rounds of consultations or into actions that will ultimately be unproductive for U.S. and Japanese interests over the long term.

Potential for U.S. Isolation. In a conflicted domestic political environment, the United States could find itself at odds with or even isolated from the other Principal States seeking to resolve the crisis, despite their substantial mistrust of and hostility toward the new DPRK leadership and its policies as those policies develop along expected and familiar lines. Managing North Korean policy with Congress has been difficult for two decades. Obtaining congressional support for outcomes judged to be less than ideal could be among the most difficult of the administration's tasks. Failure to gain strong bipartisan support for U.S. policy could undermine anything achieved diplomatically with the ROK, China, Russia, Japan, and the DPRK. The character of the U.S. approach will cause states in the region to draw conclusions about American intentions in Asia that will affect their perceptions of the value of U.S. leadership.

Japan's Response

Politics in Japan Will Be Chaotic. Tokyo will be focused on quelling public anxiety over a possible North Korean attack, protecting Japanese nationals in South Korea, monitoring Chosen Soren,[21] and dealing with boat people. Relentless Japanese demands for consultation will exhaust Washington and further marginalize Tokyo, particularly if the government asks that the United States obtain an accounting of Japanese abducted by North Korean agents in Japan to gain Japanese public support for declaring SIASJ under the 1997 Defense Guidelines. The alliance will be under strain.

Japanese Ambivalence about U.S. Military Intervention for a WMD Mission. Tokyo will hope Washington can find a way to take out North Korea's WMD and missile programs but will be concerned about China's response and the potential for a wide military conflict. The risk of military miscalculation will be significant if China and Russia put their nuclear forces on high alert due to the presence of U.S. forces close to their borders. Acknowledging the risks from U.S. military intervention is not sufficient: Washington should understand that Japan may reassess U.S. credibility as an ally and leader in Asia if the North Korean WMD programs are not eliminated. An important mitigating factor will be the extent to which Washington addresses other Japanese concerns, especially whether the United States is able to hold Chinese influence on the peninsula in check and secure a strong voice for Tokyo in determining the endstate on the peninsula.

Japan May Prefer that the United States Use UN Bases and Seek Permission Later. Using designated UN bases in Japan[22] for intervention in North Korea requires that the United States and Japan declare SIASJ under the 1997 Defense Guidelines. Making such a declaration will be problematic for Tokyo. China likely will "warn" Japan against ROK–U.S. use of these bases. Japan might prefer that the United States ask permission later, observing the thinnest formalities and simply using the UN bases as needed, without asking the Japanese to make a joint SIASJ declaration. Tokyo could then later declare that it was not given sufficient time for Diet deliberations.

Asking permission later also works to Washington's advantage given that it is not in the U.S. interest to give China the opportunity to threaten Japan. In addition, this approach would avoid a potentially prolonged Diet deliberation on SIASJ that would probably not keep pace with ROK–U.S. military operational needs. U.S. accusations that Japan is not a reliable ally would then need to be managed to prevent long-term damage to the alliance.

Russia's Response

Moscow will be under the least domestic pressure to act but will use the crisis to maximize its influence in the region while highlighting its prominent role in resolving a crisis of international dimensions. The Russians will be concerned that instability in North Korea may work to China's advantage because China has the strongest foothold in the country. Russia's posture will depend on the state of U.S.-Russia and Russia-China relations and whether siding with Washington or Beijing will improve Moscow's influence on the peninsula and in Asia, as well as its global stature. Moscow may pay lip service to U.S. WMD proliferation concerns but will stop short of supporting U.S. military intervention to secure North Korean WMD.

Russia will act to secure its 12-mile land border with North Korea and 11-mile Tumen River border to preempt refugee flows into Russia, but Moscow has no interest in playing a role in military operations inside North Korea. That calculation would change, however, if U.S. troops entered North Korea, particularly near the Russian border. In that event, Russia would likely place its nuclear forces on alert (as would China), creating the conditions for a potentially disastrous military miscalculation. It is hard to gauge how Russia would react to a Chinese military presence in North Korea; much would depend on the state of Russia-China relations and whether China was willing to consult with Russia after its intervention (Beijing is not likely to consult in advance of sending forces to North Korea).

Do the Key Findings Apply to Other Scenarios?

This study has relied on a generic scenario of regime collapse in which the decision to intervene is not an easy or obvious choice, and the primary initial goal is to contain and stabilize the situation. There are a number of studies looking at alternative scenarios of North Korean regime collapse and regime survival.[23] The type of scenario could alter the tactics of the principal states, although not their interests and goals. For instance, in a scenario in which some or even a majority of North Koreans decided to reject the institutions of the North Korean state, ROK–U.S. intervention for reunification and WMD elimination missions would seem to be more feasible politically. Responsibility-to-protect could be the starting point of an intervention that makes the transition from humanitarian to political objectives because of the existence of North Korean support for regime change or reunification. In other words, it could be argued under those conditions that North Koreans were deciding their own future for themselves, possibly easing international support for ROK–U.S. military action. However, Chinese and Russian opposition to ROK–U.S. military intervention would remain as Moscow and Beijing sought to prevent any strengthening of U.S. influence on the peninsula and in the region at their expense.

This scenario of North Korean opposition to the institutions of the current North Korean state would not alter the Key Findings in this paper. There would still be no guarantee that the North Korean state would collapse. In fact, the terrain in North Korea is well suited to a long guerrilla struggle. The United States and South Korea would still be at an informational disadvantage at the start of regime collapse compared to China, which has the largest foreign presence in North Korea and the most extensive state-to-state ties—at multiple levels and through the core institutions of the North Korean state (the party and military). Decisions on intervention that were mishandled would put U.S. interests and influence at substantial risk. More importantly, the ROK would be no more likely to support a U.S. WMD elimination mission before reunification.

Recommendations

1. U.S. Government Institutional Organization

The National Security Council (NSC) should immediately initiate a limited interagency process that brings together the core agencies: State Department, Defense Department, Central Intelligence Agency, U.S. Agency for International Development (USAID), Department of the Treasury, and Department of Energy. Representatives of these agencies (at the equivalent level of Senior Foreign Service) will comprise the Interagency Oversight Team (IOT) and periodically report to the Deputies' Committee (comprised of the Deputy Secretaries or their equivalents of each participating agency). The goal of the IOT would be to initiate a North Korea crisis planning process.

The work of the IOT should be undertaken quietly, and knowledge of the group's activities and existence should be on a need-to-know basis within the U.S. Government. As South Korea and Japan are brought into the process, the NSC, with the allies, should develop appropriate public affairs guidance explaining that the basic function of the group is to conduct diplomatic planning—to be prepared rather than because of any assessment of the likelihood of a particular event occurring. The Deputies' Committee should consider whether to share all or some of the conclusions of the IOT process with China.

Interagency Oversight Team Tasks.

- Decide the composition of small working groups to tackle significant functional issues that would arise in a contingency: WMD elimination, humanitarian response, legal basis for actions, alliance relations, and policy options—operational and strategic.

- Task the Intelligence Community to develop regular updates of the Principal States' concerns and interests with respect to North Korea, producing a series of papers assessing the situation, outlining possible steps, and setting up checklists of issues to be considered.

- Develop and disseminate the procedures for the small working groups and functions they are expected to fulfill.

Functional Group Tasks. The IOT should task the five functional groups.

WMD Elimination Group Tasks: seizure and control of WMD, seizure and control of fissile material yet to be weaponized, securing scientists involved in these programs, actions to close exits, and actions to reinvigorate the Proliferation Security Initiative.

The first three tasks occur in North Korea and span the entire process of locating, characterizing, neutralizing, removing, and destroying WMD. This process includes the destruction of weapons and related programs, as well as the physical infrastructure and the securing of WMD-related scientists. WMD elimination will entail a geographically dispersed hunt for potential WMD sites in an environment where North Korean forces are likely to oppose U.S. efforts. It is an undertaking that will require planning for security, logistics, transportation, and other enabling capabilities. The WMD Elimination Group will decide the composition of assessment teams and their needs.

Accurate intelligence of course will be an enormous asset. Early engagement with the International Atomic Energy Agency will be important. The group should work with the Legal Frameworks team to consider the legal authorities necessary to initiate WMD elimination operations—presumably this will require a UN Security Council resolution establishing an international authority to eliminate North Korea's WMD programs. This resolution will make reference to all past UN resolutions on North Korean WMD issues, which together form a powerful political rationale for addressing the threat the North Korean programs pose to the international community. The group will work with the Operational Policy Options team on the necessary diplomatic actions at the UN.

Humanitarian Response Group Tasks: antipandemic planning, food distribution, shelter and clothing, and sanitation and clean water. The Humanitarian Response Group will make an initial assessment of likely needs and integrate relevant U.S. organizations—Centers for Disease Control, USAID, State, Health and Human Services—into planning efforts.

Pandemic planning will be critical given the incidence of multidrug-resistant tuberculosis (TB) in North Korea. Based on World Health Organization estimates for 2009, North Korea has the highest rate of TB in the world outside of sub-Saharan Africa: an incidence rate of 345 cases per 100,000. TB is highly infectious and deadly. Half of those who go untreated die, and because of exposures to others, each case may spawn between 10 and 20 new cases. The bacteria does not respect borders. For instance, multidrug-resistant strains that arrived in Russia following the fall of the Soviet Union have turned up in Western Europe, the Middle East, and South Africa.[24]

Legal Frameworks Group Tasks: review existing legal instruments and determine how they could come into play in a Korean contingency. How should the United States position itself with respect to each of the documents listed below? Additionally, this group should engage Seoul at the earliest possible opportunity, since the ROK may take the lead on a number of efforts. The legal instruments include the following:

- ROK constitution (Article III)

- DPRK constitution

- UN Security Council Resolutions 83, 84, 85 (from the Korean War)

- UN Security Council Resolutions 1674, 1738, and 1706 (responsibility-to-protect)

- UN Security Council Resolutions 1970 and 1973 (Libya) and 1975 (Ivory Coast)

- UN General Assembly Resolution 195 of December 12, 1948 (recognizes ROK as the sole legitimate government of Korea)

- UN Charter Chapter 7, Article 42 (restoring international peace)

- UN Charter Chapter 7, Article 51 (self-defense, refugees, WMD, safety of ROK citizens in DPRK)

- The Armistice

- 1961 China-DPRK Security Treaty

- 2000 Russia-DPRK Friendship Treaty

- U.S.-Japan Security Treaty; 1997 Defense Guidelines (SIASJ)

- U.S.–ROK Security Treaty

- Inter-Korean Agreements

- Six Party Talks understandings.

Operational Policy Options Group Tasks: translate policy decisions into achievable diplomatic steps; map the actions the United States must take, in which venues, and through what mechanisms. This group will focus on:

- humanitarian relief

- stabilization

- WMD elimination.

Strategic Policy Options Group Tasks: this group will consider broad strategic issues:

- management of the contingency at the UN Security Council

- lead role of the ROK

■ alliance management issues/conflicting national priorities

■ areas for U.S.-China cooperation: examine existing dialogues, especially the Strategic and Economic Dialogue, for ways to integrate North Korea issues such as pandemic planning; stable command and control over North Korean WMD; economic reform in the DPRK—graduating North Korea from humanitarian to development aid; and corridors for humanitarian intervention

■ acceptable endstates of intervention.

This group should consider how to prevent a major disruption in U.S.-China relations, and how to manage alliance relations with South Korea and Japan during the crisis. Finding areas for "soft" cooperation with China—on pandemic planning, for instance—will be important to keeping Sino-American relations stable. The goal will be to try to engage China early and often.

This group will consider the strategic and diplomatic implications of an intervention that stabilizes North Korea and under what conditions this would be acceptable to the United States and the other principal states. A particular focus will be on how to manage alliance relationships if outcomes are less than optimal—defined as the continuation of both a divided peninsula and a North Korean state with WMD programs under some form of international monitoring.

2. International Institutional Organization

Once the U.S. Government is organized internally, the appropriate agency members of the IOT should initiate quiet discussions with appropriate counterparts in international organizations such as the World Bank and Asian Development Bank (State and Treasury), the World Food Program, United Nations Children's Fund, the UN High Commission on Refugees, the International Organization for Migration (State and USAID), and the International Atomic Energy Agency (State and Energy).

3. U.S.–Republic of Korea Coordination

The IOT will direct State to initiate quiet consultations with South Korea briefed to the IOT. It is not likely that South Korea will share its plans and thinking fully with the United States. However, successful intervention or political management of a North Korean contingency will require close U.S.–ROK communication and coordination.

4. U.S.–Republic of Korea–Japan Coordination

The United States and South Korea should reach out to Japan to take the measure of Japanese internal thinking on instability/collapse in North Korea. There are a range of opinions on North Korean collapse within the Japanese Foreign Ministry and between the Foreign Ministry and other agencies such as the Ministry of Defense, the Cabinet Secretariat, and the Cabinet Intelligence and Research Office.

5. U.S.–ROK–Japan–China–Russia Coordination

Both the United States and South Korea will want to meet with the other principal states under the rubric of the Six Party Talks (minus North Korea) to project the regional nature of their approach and in order to coordinate pandemic planning and other cooperative initiatives. While the United States and South Korea will attempt to discuss substantive political issues in this venue, China is not likely to cooperate.

Conclusion

Regime collapse in North Korea would challenge the best political leaders in its complexity and in its potential to shift the strategic landscape in Asia in ways inimical to U.S. national security interests. The odds are decidedly against the regime collapsing. If it did, however, the ensuing crisis would be extremely dangerous and easily susceptible to escalation beyond North Korea's borders. Much would need to go right in order to prevent a wider conflict from engulfing the region. This study attempts to identify what would need to go right by examining the political interests and diplomatic challenges that regime collapse in North Korea could bring into play among the United States, South Korea, Japan, China, North Korea, and Russia.

The dilemmas Washington would face are perhaps best underscored by the finding in this study that regime collapse does not mean state collapse, at least not in the short run. Any intervention, therefore, would be problematic. The international community will oppose actions seeking to dissolve the North Korean state coercively without the support of a North Korean majority. Even if the regime's writ did not extend to every province, China has consistently demonstrated that it has a strategic stake in the continuation of the North Korean state and Beijing would presumably act to protect that stake.

This study concludes that North Korean cooperation will be more critical to the achievement of U.S. and ROK goals than has previously been appreciated. If cooperation is withheld, it is hard to imagine that Washington and Seoul could achieve WMD elimination or reunification, let alone humanitarian intervention. The United States and South Korea will not operate in a political vacuum. While both will seek to be the primary actors in a North Korean regime collapse crisis, the actions of China and North Korea will profoundly influence their decisions. The cooperation of Japan and Russia, as well as the support of the United Nations, will be critically important to the achievement of a politically acceptable and stable outcome.

While wrestling with difficult and momentous decisions regarding intervention and the endstate on the peninsula, domestic politics in the United States and South Korea will be conflicted over how to proceed in the crisis. Politics in Washington, in particular, could undermine anything achieved diplomatically with South Korea, Japan, China, Russia, and North Korea. In addition, unmet expectations by the Republic of Korea and Japan could damage U.S. relationships with these two allies. The potential for adversarial relations with China post-crisis will be equally high.

In this dynamic and complex environment, the realism, finesse, and effectiveness of Washington's approach to regime collapse in North Korea could well determine the future of U.S. leadership in Asia. It is therefore essential to consider today how best to position the U.S. Government to respond intelligently to what would surely be the most serious challenge America has faced in Asia since the Vietnam War.

Notes

[1] M.I. Finley, *History of the Peloponnesian War*, trans. Rex Warner (New York: Penguin Books, 1972), 122.

[2] The authors conducted interviews with former U.S. and Republic of Korea (ROK) officials and with experts in Seoul (April and October 2010), in Beijing (May 2011), and in the United States (in New York in November 2010, at Stanford University in January 2011, and in Washington, DC, in November 2010 and January 2011). They had discussions with Japanese experts and former Japanese officials in Tokyo (April 2010), in Seoul (October 2010), and in Washington, DC (May 2011). They also met with Chinese experts and former officials in Beijing (May 2011).

[3] A few studies leave out Russia, or both Russia and Japan, considering them to be marginal players in a North Korean regime collapse crisis. We believe it is a mistake to exclude either state, especially since the advent of the Six Party Talks process in late 2003, but also for the specific reasons cited above. Interestingly, well before the Six Party Talks were created, a ROK military officer wrote a study on regime collapse that included all six states. See Moo Bong Ryoo, "The ROK Army's Role When North Korea Collapses Without a War with the ROK," published by the School of Advanced Military Studies, U.S. Army Command and General Staff College, Fort Leavenworth, KS, January 2001.

[4] The revised 1997 U.S.-Japan Defense Guidelines redefined *U.S.-Japan defense cooperation* as: (1) cooperation under normal circumstances; (2) action in response to an armed attack against Japan; and (3) cooperation in Situations in Areas Surrounding Japan (SIASJ) that will have an important influence on Japan's peace and security. See General Noboru Yamaguchi, "Thoughts about the Japan-U.S. Alliance after the Transformation, With a Focus on International Peace Cooperation Activities," *The National Institute for Defense Studies News*, no. 96 (January 2006), 2.

[5] Among the most significant differences: unlike West and East Germany, South and North Korea fought a bloody war with each other; West and East Germany established diplomatic relations nearly two decades prior to reunification, while the two Koreas not only do not recognize each other as sovereign states, but also their constitutions each claim sovereignty over the entire Korean Peninsula; and East Germany had no latitude in its foreign policy as a Soviet satellite state, while North Korea appears to have considerable independence from China.

[6] Authors' interviews with Chinese experts and former officials, May 23–27, 2011, in Beijing.

[7] Despite periodic reports that China is reviewing its North Korea policy, and that there is increasing debate over the DPRK's value as a strategic buffer zone, and even online surveys in China suggesting a majority of respondents believe North Korea undermines China's national and security interests, this debate appears to have had only a limited impact on Chinese policy. See Scott Snyder, "China's Nuclear North Korea Fever," *Comparative Connections*, October 2009.

[8] Influential Chinese analyst Shen Dingli argues that "even if China would not ask for it, a nuclear North Korea's ability to pin down U.S. forces in a Taiwan Strait contingency deters America's consideration of possible military intervention.... [T]his is the link between North Korea and Taiwan." See "North Korea's Strategic Significance to China," *China Security* (Autumn 2006), 21.

⁹ See Park Changhee, "North Korean Contingency and Prospects of China's Military Intervention," Ilmin International Relations Institute Working Paper Series No. 5, October 2010, for a good discussion of Chinese strategy.

¹⁰ Japan's concerns are strategic: Tokyo has based its security policy on the assumption of a divided peninsula, and is concerned that reunification might drive Korea closer to China. In addition, a U.S. presence in Japan is closely linked to the existence of a similar presence in the ROK. See International Crisis Group, "Japan and North Korea: Bones of Contention," *Asia Report* no. 100 (June 27, 2005).

¹¹ For a good discussion of Russia-North Korea relations, see Alexander Vorontsov, "Current Russia-North Korea Relations: Challenges and Achievements," Brookings Institution, February 2007. Vorontsov maintains that the security of the Russian Far East would be affected by an armed confrontation in North Korea, and that the presence of U.S. military forces near the Russian and Chinese borders would cause elevated tensions and risk a wider conflict.

¹² Ibid.

¹³ For a discussion of the various possible legal justifications for intervention and stabilization, see Shin Beomchul, "A Review of the Legalities Associated with a Sudden Change in North Korea," Ilmin International Relations Institute Working Paper Series No. 6, October 2010 (sponsored by the MacArthur Foundation's Asia Security Initiative).

¹⁴ Security Council Resolution 85 of July 31, 1950, "requests the Unified Command to exercise responsibility for determining the requirements for the relief and support of the civilian population of Korea and for establishing in the field the procedures for providing such relief and support." The term "Korea" is ambiguous in the text and contrasts with the use of "Republic of Korea" and "North Korea" elsewhere in this and other Security Council resolutions during the Korean War.

¹⁵ United Nations (UN) Charter, Article 2, paragraph 7.

¹⁶ Paragraphs 138–139 of this document (UN General Assembly, September 15, 2005, A/60/L.1) state the following:

> *Responsibility to protect populations from genocide, war crimes, ethnic cleansing and crimes against humanity. 138. Each individual State has the responsibility to protect its populations from genocide, war crimes, ethnic cleansing and crimes against humanity. This responsibility entails the prevention of such crimes, including their incitement, through appropriate and necessary means. We accept that responsibility and will act in accordance with it. The international community should, as appropriate, encourage and help States to exercise this responsibility and support the United Nations in establishing an early warning capability. 139. The international community, through the United Nations, also has the responsibility to use appropriate diplomatic, humanitarian and other peaceful means, in accordance with Chapters VI and VIII of the Charter, to help protect populations from genocide, war crimes, ethnic cleansing and crimes against humanity. In this context, we are prepared to take collective action, in a timely and decisive manner, through the Security Council, in accordance with the Charter, including Chapter VII, on a case-by-case basis and in cooperation with relevant regional organizations as appropriate, should peaceful means be inadequate and national authorities manifestly*

fail to protect their populations from genocide, war crimes, ethnic cleansing and crimes against humanity. We stress the need for the General Assembly to continue consideration of the responsibility to protect populations from genocide, war crimes, ethnic cleansing and crimes against humanity and its implications, bearing in mind the principles of the Charter and international law. We also intend to commit ourselves, as necessary and appropriate, to helping States build capacity to protect their populations from genocide, war crimes, ethnic cleansing and crimes against humanity and to assisting those which are under stress before crises and conflicts break out.

[17] For a review and discussion of responsibility-to-protect, see Christoph Mikulaschek, "The United Nations Security Council and the Responsibility to Protect: Policy, Process, and Practice," Report from the 39th International Peace Institute Vienna Seminar on Peacemaking and Peacekeeping, available at <http://responsibilitytoprotect.org/mikulaschekpdf>.

[18] Ibid., 23.

[19] Xinhua carried a report on the Russian statement on March 19, 2011, and on the Chinese statement on March 20, 2011.

[20] During the authors' May 23–27, 2011, meetings in Beijing, Chinese interlocutors expressed concern over what they perceive to be exaggerated claims by average South Koreans to Korean historical achievements. These Chinese interlocutors also noted that South Korean tourists to Mount Paektu at the China/North Korea border also tend to take pictures holding the South Korean flag—suggesting a Korean territorial claim. For their part, Koreans have historically opposed an expansion of Chinese influence on the peninsula.

[21] Chosen Soren is a pro-North Korea organization composed of Korean expatriates living in Japan.

[22] Seven U.S. military bases in Japan are designated as United Nations Command bases. The UN Command–Japan Status of Forces Agreement of 1954 formalized this arrangement. These bases are: Yokota Air Base (Air Force), Camp Zama (Army), Sasebo (Navy), Yokosuka (Navy), Kadena (Air Force), Futenma (Marine Corps), and White Beach (Navy). See Colonel Jung Won-il, Republic of Korea Army, "The Future of the United Nations Command in the Republic of Korea," Strategy Research Project (Carlisle Barracks, PA: U.S. Army War College, May 3, 2004), 5–6.

[23] For a brief overview of recent studies, see See-Won Byun, "North Korea Contingency Planning and U.S.–ROK Cooperation" (Center for U.S.-Korea Policy at the Asia Foundation, September 2009).

[24] See a discussion of the problem by Sharon Perry, Heidi Linton, and Gary Schoolnik, "Tuberculosis in North Korea," *Science* (January 21, 2011), 283.

Acknowledgments

The authors wish to thank the many experts on the Korean Peninsula in the United States, the Republic of Korea, China, and Japan who shared their insights and perspectives with us. They helped us think through the implications of regime collapse in North Korea and frame the questions that will confront policymakers. We also benefited from the suggestions of many reviewers of early drafts of this paper, all of them former U.S. Government officials from various agencies and levels of government who have spent time working on North Korea. We will not name them in order to protect their anonymity, but we are deeply grateful for their expert advice. We are grateful to our peer reviewers, Bob Sutter and Bruce Klingner, also experts on the region, who took the time to comment extensively on later drafts of the paper. At National Defense University, Nicholas Rostow, Phillip Saunders, and Michael Mazaar provided useful comments and recommendations on structure and substance that resulted in a better final product. Daniel Kim deserves special thanks for his extraordinary research skills. He and Saori Takahashi kept us abreast of breaking news and undertook a number of special research projects that helped us develop our analysis. They are both excellent Research Assistants.

About the Authors

Ferial Ara Saeed is an American diplomat on detail from the Department of State to the Center for Strategic Research in the Institute for National Strategic Studies. She was Deputy Director of the State Department's Korea Desk from 2001 to 2004. North Asia is her primary area of diplomatic expertise, especially U.S. foreign policy toward China, Japan, and the Korean Peninsula. She has served on the China and Japan Desks at the State Department, at the U.S. Embassy in Tokyo, and on the Asian Affairs staff of the National Security Council. Early in her diplomatic career, she had assignments to the Middle East and covered the region as an analyst in the Bureau of Intelligence and Research. She is the author of *Redefining Success: Applying Lessons in Nuclear Diplomacy from North Korea to Iran* (National Defense University Press, September 2010). Ms. Saeed's academic background is in the Middle East and Southwest Asia. She holds an M.A. in International Affairs from Columbia University and a B.A. in Political Science and Anthropology from the University of California at Berkeley.

James J. Przystup is a Senior Fellow at the Center for Strategic Research in the Institute for National Strategic Studies and Director of the Trans-Pacific Forum at National Defense University. Throughout his career, Dr. Przystup has worked on issues related to the Asia-Pacific region: as a staff member of the House of Representatives Subcommittee on Asian and Pacific Affairs; at the IBM World Trade Corporation; as Deputy Director of the Presidential Commission on U.S.-Japan Relations; on the Policy Planning Staff at the Department of State; on the Policy Planning Staff in the Office of the Secretary of Defense; and as Director of the Asian Studies Center at The Heritage Foundation. He holds a B.A., summa cum laude, from the University of Detroit, and an M.A. in International Relations and Ph.D. in History from the University of Chicago.